SWIMS

Elizabeth-Jane Burnett is a poet and academic with a focus on innovative poetics. She holds a BA in English from Oxford, an MA and PhD in Contemporary Poetics from Royal Holloway, University of London, and studied performance at the Bowery Poetry Club in New York and Naropa. Creative publications include *oh-zones*, *Her Body: The City*, *Exotic Birds* and *M* (a poem-film about John Clare with artist Brian Shields). Her work has been anthologised in *Dear World and Everyone In It: New Poetry in the UK* (Bloodaxe, 2013) and *Out of Everywhere 2: Linguistically Innovative Poetry by Women in North America and the UK* (Reality Street, 2015). She curates ecopoetics exhibitions and is Senior Lecturer in Creative Writing at Newman University in Birmingham.

Swims

Elizabeth-Jane Burnett

Penned in the Margins

LONDON

PUBLISHED BY PENNED IN THE MARGINS
Toynbee Studios, 28 Commercial Street, London E1 6AB
www.pennedinthemargins.co.uk

All rights reserved
© Elizabeth-Jane Burnett

The right of Elizabeth-Jane Burnett to be identified as the author of this work has been asserted by her in accordance with Section 77 of the Copyright, Designs and Patent Act 1988.

This book is in copyright. Subject to statutory exception and to provisions of relevant collective licensing agreements, no reproduction of any part may take place without the written permission of Penned in the Margins.

First published 2017
This edition 2019

Printed by Lightning Source

ISBN
978-1-908058-49-2

This book is sold subject to the condition that it shall not, by way of trade or otherwise, be lent, re-sold, hired out, or otherwise circulated without the publisher's prior consent in any form of binding or cover other than that in which it is published and without a similar condition including this condition being imposed on the subsequent purchaser.

CONTENTS

PREFACE   15

I   *Devon*   The Teign   19
II   *Somerset*   The Barle   23
III   *Sussex*   The Ouse   25
IV   *Sussex*   The Ouse   29
V   *Cumbria*   Grasmere   37
VI   *London*   Hampstead Heath   41
VII   *London*   King's Cross Pond   47

POEMS FOR MY FATHER
                       Aegina   49
                       The Voice   50
                       Wallflowers   51

VIII   *Snowdonia*   Llyn Gwynant   53
IX   *Snowdonia*   Llyn Idwal   55
X   *Sussex*   The English Channel   57
XI   *Cornwall*   Porthmeor   61
XII   *Devon*   The Dart   63

AUTHOR'S NOTE

Swims is a long poem documenting twelve wild swims across England and Wales, beginning and ending in Devon, my home county, and moving through Somerset, Surrey, the Lake District, London, Snowdonia, Sussex and Cornwall. Each swim is conceived as an environmental action, testing the ways in which individuals might effect environmental change. They are interrupted by a sequence for my father, whose health deteriorated during the writing of the poem; part of this sequence features swimming in the Aegean Sea.

Parts of *Swims* have been displayed in The Trembling Grass, an exhibition I curated with the Centre for Contemporary Art and the Natural World (CCANW) in 2014 at the Innovation Centre, University of Exeter. This also showcased work from poets such as Allen Fisher, Maggie O'Sullivan and Harriet Tarlo. Excerpts have been performed at the Flow and Fracture conference, ULB, Brussels (2014); Warwick Thursdays (2015), run by Jonathan Skinner at Warwick University; and at the Language, Landscape and the Sublime symposium at Dartington Hall (2016) — where I also curated a group swim in the Dart — and The Barrel House, Totnes (2016). 'Swim XI, The English Channel' was performed at the Sussex Poetry Festival, June 6, 2015, and engages with *Swallows and Amazons*.

'Swim XIII, King's Cross Pond' was published in *Lighthouse* (II: Winter

2016 — an ecopoetics edition guest-edited by Anna Reckin); 'Swim I, The Teign' has been published in *The Learned Pig* (2016) and 'Preface' and 'Swim III, The Ouse' have been published in *The Clearing* (2016). *Swims* is the subject of my article 'Swims: Body, Ritual, Erasure as Environmental Activism,' in *Jacket 2* (Fall 2015). The Poetry Society published a section of 'Preface' in a feature by Jen Hadfield on nature poetry, 'Ways to be Wilder' (2016).

For my father, who taught me to swim.

Swims

'A dictionary would start from the point at which it would no longer give the meanings but the tasks of words.' — BATAILLE

§

To Swim To give
up.
To disappear.
To appear
in *Vanity Fair* before breakfast.
To afterwards destroy economy of Greece.[1]
To float.
To pierce film lid between air and water.
To explode outwards.
To be an assemblage.
To flower
in the wrong place to be in the wrong
   place.
To drift.
To not advance capitalism.
To grow in a hedge.
To be lichen.
To be at once
in the body
and under
and over it.
To sink
and to get back up.
To spread tail feather

in display of bone
to be closer to skeleton and totally fine
what's the worst that could happen
already fallen
already wet
already missing
from the earth but recoverable always
there is something left
to be dug up
to be eaten
to be stolen
there is something left always when words are at
their fullest stretch
something left that cannot be taken.
To not being taken.

[1] Christine Lagard, Director of the International Monetary Fund, explains how she starts the day with swimming in 'Christine Lagard: Et si c'etait elle?' — *Vanity Fair France*, December 2014.

PREFACE

Swimming is continuous. Only the rivers are intermittent.

The river is something that happens
like exercise or illness to the body
on any given day I am rivering.

Not that   *the river is like* the body
or   *the river is* the body
but   both have gone
and what is left is something else.

To not end where you thought you did
not with skin but water
not with arms but meadow
of watercress, dropwort, floating pennywort
against all odds to be buoyant.

To feel there is an upward force
greater than the weight of the heart
the knuckles the head to feel as in to feel
it physically push up the ribs which are bones now

everything remembering what it is
becoming is remembering
sinking in the silt is the sand
of the shell of the bone singing

in the reeds in the rushes
hordes of heartbeats not my own:

mollusc onto stone
milfoil onto moss
mayfly onto trout

metal onto clay
acid onto wire
electrified chicken wire to keep the salmon in
the summer we'll make a day of it
fill the car up, make a day of it
fill the river, make like mayflies

in the summer, swim
in traffic, swim in the car
in the river in the summer in the city
in the chicken in the acid in the salmon in the rain
in the silt in the sulphur in the algae in the day we'll come
and part as friends

in the day in the river in the moss in the rushes we'll come and part

in the river in the heather in the rushes in the rain we'll stay and the
day and the day
and the days dart over and summer is over
us salmon leap over
us all come apart
in the end

of the day
and the river.

I

THE TEIGN

'A major source of pollution is the disused barytes mine at Bridford, and in July 1962 an effluent from these premises containing toxic quantities of dissolved metals and free sulphuric acid killed large numbers of fish in the length of river downstream of the Rookery Brook as far as Preston.' — RIVER TEIGN FISHERIES SURVEY

1. Lay River Teign Fisheries Survey along river bank.

2. Enter river with a set of problems.

3. Think about each problem in turn.

4. When no longer thinking about the problem, consider it dissolved.

5. At the point of each dissolution, insert the problem into the survey.

	Salmon	Sea Trout
1951	118	592
1952	45	**this is not solving anything**

Biological examination of this area has shown that **I am too old**, there are very large numbers of nymphs and larvae of several species present and together with the material drifting down with the current and the terrestrial insects falling in off the trees there should be sufficient food for a fish population to thrive.

Since the experiment **may not make any difference** a report on each year's work will be prepared for general circulation.

Molluscs and Crustaceans are very rare indeed, although isolated pockets of **guilt** do occur and in some of the tributaries, particularly the River Wray, it is quite common.

SAMPLING TECHNIQUES

For the purpose of the survey it was decided to ignore the 'How Is This Helping', i.e. fish hatched in the spring of 1963 since because of their small size they were difficult to capture and equally difficult to identify as trout or salmon.

NB. It is unfortunate that **I don't have enough time** in surveys of this nature to distinguish between juvenile brown trout and those fish which will eventually migrate to sea as sea trout smolts. * In some waters it is possible to recognise what appear to be different 'types' of trout parrs e.g. some have more slender wrists and more gracefully forked tails than others, but it is not known for certain that **I should do more**. In fact the results on the Teign rather indicate that **I should do less** as such fish were not at all common and yet the Teign is well known as an excellent sea trout river.

This report is arranged in four sections as follows

A. INTRODUCTION

B. METHODS

C. RESULTS

D. APPENDIX (containing **Fukushima**)

In its upper reaches the main river flows for much of its course through dense deciduous woodland and the stretch between The **Arctic** and Steps Bridge is particularly noteworthy in this respect. Beyond Dunsford the surrounding catchment is predominantly open pasture land, although there are patches of **migraine**, and even in the open fields there is often a belt of trees along the river banks. There are isolated industrial migraines on this length of river, e.g. the concrete works and quarry at Trusham and the now disused barytes mine at Bridford, although just north of Newton Abbot the river passes through a considerable concentration of **timetabling**. Beyond this the river skirts the town of Newton Abbot and finally opens out into a relatively narrow estuary down which it flows to Teignmouth and **what if I sink** the English Channel.

II

THE BARLE

The Barle creases land between stitches
the earth has gathered into hills.

We enter here, along the fold, cut water
with the scream that pours from us,

cold and clear and bodied,
follow the will of the current down,

past bumps of trout and damselflies,
swallow sweet spasms of buttercups

where the sun spots us under
the surface, falling faster,

legs against rock, knee-knocked,
as in Fukushima, where fishermen

record radioactive caesium in fish,
three years after the earthquake,

three years on from the tsunami:
I can no more take this out

of the poem as out of the water.
A flock of starlings floats above,

suspended, like oil in vinegar,
marking stillness

where there should be flight,
treading water.

Drop after drop,

they make the sky
a spill of purring tar.

Though we leave the water,
there is no emergence.

III

THE OUSE

The site of Virginia Woolf's drowning. Poem performed at increasing speed.

'The simplest method of determining the velocity of a current involves an observer, a floating object or drifter, and a timing device.' – US DEPARTMENT OF COMMERCE, NATIONAL OCEANIC AND ATMOSPHERIC ADMINISTRATION[1]

One by one the horses come.

Breath's soft shuffle through
water foams open and out
purrs a language
I am learning

through the body
I am learning
through the fact
of my being here
haunch in water
standing
head in hedge
standing
with everything I've got.

The simplest method of determining the velocity of a current involves a horse, a floating object or drifter and a timing device.

One by one the horses come purring
me open I stir and shake
shivers jolt in parts
of the body yet to be discovered
I ache in the hedge
of the water
is forcing me open
the horses are dark as the earth
darker than earth
deeper
their flanks rise from the pit
of the word the gut of the word
the ditch the dust the ear
the éar the eard
the native soil or land
deeper than that is the horse
that purrs me open
in water
in open
in open water

the simplest method of determining the velocity of a word
involves a horse, a girl and a timing device.

One by one the horses come stirring me open
into water into open water
I bend and purr

from rib to hip is a rich loaming
I flank and fall
and purr in the water I am learning
that the simplest method of determining the velocity of a word
involves a horse, a girl and a poem.

[1] 'Currents: How are currents measured?' U.S Department of Commerce, National Oceanic and Atmospheric Administration. Revised 25th March 2008. Web. Accessed 12.9.14.

IV

THE OUSE

'I'll be doing a swim wearing a swimsuit on which I've written some hopes and fears on current environmental issues. I'm inviting you to write your own hopes and fears on my swimsuit which I will take with me as I swim, writing the water with our collective thoughts. Your writing can be as brief or long as you like, as the space of the swimsuit permits. You may have a few lines, or a single word. I may sink with the weight of them or rise with their purpose.' — EMAIL TO COLLABORATORS

suit-text before water   **suit-text after water**

sun slides buttery over the rushes
water softens and stills

elsewhere, events

I, the rhythm of river
part-nature, part-poem, part-kin

GAZA

May you not be a war   I, the collaboration

zone   part nature — parts nature   *May you not be a war*
collapses   *zone*

the shoulders, falls back onto milk
I, Cleopatra
with sun's areola flush across throat

I, the event
individual forges collective afloat

submerged in the matter
of all of us mattering

Does my carbon
footprint look big in this?

athrob exit river
to laughter's warm shiver

I brim with love for the parts that need
I, the brim of the river
I brim the world from this spot out
to be to be to be outwards
I brim outwards to it:

nettles nettles rush
lemon loosestrife thyme
purple loosestrife flood
lemon flood purple flood
in Dawlish   flood   in Mosul
cannot compare   cannot compass
compassion compressed
as flowers through pages of a book
to look
doesn't do
much
looking back we see the frailty through
the years the pages

press Mosul
in the river banks
and look and look and not to look
        away

    warm the eyes
    vein the lids
    push to the tip
    of the lash the light
"Kurdish forces push front lines
     low hills brim

sending smoke into the sky," he says
    I brim
can he do more
         than report
can I do more
         than read
    read into the river raw with teeth
    read with teeth.

Body crackles with distortion
       static of river heaves
body through
       stays / moves
the same
       but reconfigured
   as if to say perhaps
the person

                              has a fractal
        relation
                              to the river
        as hydrogen — hydrogen — oxygen perhaps
                body — body — river
                imagine every full stop
                replaced by perhaps
                that is a language
                I would like to live in perhaps

        Deep in the water a blue so unlike blue you think of almost
        every other colour first perhaps yellow perhaps brown
        perhaps flotilla of speckled wood
butterflies   explode on the tongue   perhaps perhaps perhaps
        (an ellipsis) You   swallow   and there
        is nothing to hold on to   your throat is a gutter
        for the fallen yes

        Your jaw locks yes Instead of perhaps a yes A stoplight
        loosejaw is its own torch emitting red light as well as blue
        yes Blue is rarely just blue yes
           River rarely just river yes   Body rarely just body yes
        Think of all the things I've swallowed
                like a ceasefire
                like a widening of the territory
                like an open-ended truce.

        Back re-orientates itself to water   in a new way of
                                                  walking

a new way of moving on the earth   to drift like wood
in water   with such soft rooting   glimpse a pine
cone before it is one   see it green   hanging bunched
like bananas   forget what you know of texture   what it is
to be hard brittle starts soft why not be soft choose to live
with softness   as far as nature   chooses
genetics give us   the invitation to be ourselves why not
      accept
push up, up, to the top of ourselves   push out of our lungs
up through the larynx, the ceiling, the cortex, the feathers

               I place my palms to your bark and pulse
pulse through the matter and up I up and begin to sense
       distance differently
impossibly far is here galaxies here and to be that tall and
       distant yet
consistently you all the way up from navel to stars up I up
       like a soft soaring
rooted

                    we glide
a moving forest all committed   what more are tribes
villages of poems pulsating together   not always
perfectly but sometimes sometimes there is a perfect pulse
and people ring in chords layer on layer on layer we
breathe and sound simultaneous and why not speak these
chords at times when there is no time breathe at
times when there is no time sound at times when there is

no time for speech or breath or sound are here and only
the time you are given for the tasks you are given is
the time you receive though you know it is no gift

                                        so to swim
is the time to swim as much as it is anything and legs
and heads seem far from time but are as much it as it is
            anything   and so to swim is to bring
the body back   from wherever it has been   in time

                                        so to swim
            is to be in time not on it

a field tears itself from the earth like a strip of velcro
                re-attaches
to the retinas and glows   glows through the eyelids   veins
are clouded   gold sifts and puffs

jellyfish   eyes are immense: *jellyfish*

double, triple the size of on land   head is light cloud eye
is immense golden trafficking colour is everywhere how
            light is your head is
the opposite of migraine: there is gold pouring from your

head it is the
brightest light you have ever owned it pours from you

and it is like speaking
when lips part   and tongue chimes   against roof of river
        mouth
opens
yellow bubbles of light fall in   open vowels little twigs of
        words open
edges   at the edge of words opening

and speech comes swifts
circle and little throbs   of letters tumble   and I can hear
their hearts beating   little throbs of words beating and smell of
        fur and
feathers wet on the wing of words wetting the air tongue wet on
        the air
beating
little wild words thump in the mouth.

V

GRASMERE

'As soon as I come to Grasmere, I shall begin to teach you all the things which I know that I think you would like to know: one thing will be swimming.' — THOMAS DE QUINCEY

A snatched one
a clipped one
a bootleg
         I run. Past the boathouses, padlocks, holiday homes.
         I run. I have to get there.
                 A step into silver
    the last of the light and under
    I under me
    all the lost things
    bits of lost time and heart
    preserved as pebbles under
    I under me every torn day
    everything taken is temporary

lake as repository   for everything stolen
         each follicle, each beat missed
         lies under I under
         water lick
         drop on lip
         trickle slip of body
         not calibrated about to fall off

the edge of the world
effluent from every hotel
inside me four years
on from tsunami
Canadian fishermen report
"waist-high" debris from Fukushima
for 15 miles in the Pacific "It's incredible,
piles and piles. Drift nets up there with catastrophic death
in them… The currents are big, bringing everything in."

Though we leave that body
there is no emergence.
There is no other body.

Silverlimbed
              I rise.
Polished by last light. Flash of back and cheek.
                       I rise and run   back into time   from
the snatched one
the clipped one
the bootleg
              still playing.

[return]   Man pulls fish
             across floor
             in last dance of night.
             Catches her throat
             white as a bone
             and her body
             as it hangs there
             limp but luminous
             is something like a wish.

Resentment at his being there
into gift of my being there
to see it, the moment
another world
broke the surface
into this one
its lithe neck one long stretch
of wildness
wondering if we'd touched
when I was the wrong one
in the wrong world
if she had watched me
from a distance.

A difficult swim. A snatched one, a clipped one, from a timetable
too regulated. A timetable takes something from you that is hard to
recover. It believes you can be reduced to a model of yourself that is
flat, made from paper or plastic, or that an online version of you can
be downloaded. It believes it can work with an outline of you, with

all the guts emptied out, all the mess, all human circuitry.

And so to swim is
to explode column width of day's database, expand with joy in the
margins, find and replace total with ethic with heart.

Is to be where people had not planned you to be.
No barcode as body passes over water. Here they lose your scent and
there is panic in the spreadsheets.

You are something
untraceable having finished the public performance of you, here you
exist unticketed. Here you bark in the wetness of fur in the tickle of
light you are forged as lake glows copper on Bunsen burner you are
shining newly.

If I took this version of myself,
laid it out like a fish on a desk; wild in the eye and the hair and the
skin; burning through with myself. There would be no place for me.

VI

HAMPSTEAD HEATH

1. Go for a swim in the rain.

2. For each individual raindrop seen or felt, take the name of a
   Fukushima resident seeking compensation from Tepco.

3. Collect a stone from the bottom of the pond and write the name
   on it.

4. Write in response to the stone.

5. Return the stone to the water.

§

1. Rain stops a minute before entering the pond.

2. Names almost entirely absent from Fukushima reports, mostly a
   nameless "one woman" who is quoted.

3. There are no stones, only mud.

4. As I start to think about the one name I have, a new couple enter
   the pond. They are loudly in love and I cannot focus.

5. I try again to think about the name as I write it on a twig but a
    man is talking to me — "Who would have thought the sun
    would come out?" I write the name on one side, the man's
    words on the other. I push the twig into the water.

§

Wake with water
in mouth,
tongue coated
in moss,
the skull a birdcage,
robin and wren pulse
through its shell an oyster
of feathery pearls.
"Can you whistle?"
"Whistle, Ma'am?"
"I want you to whistle to my bullfinches,"
on the tongue, a strawberry
                    a story
          a history
      of open-throated thrushes
trickle out a cast of Hardy characters
my tongue is coated in England
a hawk batters my cheeks
breaks out my face
beats up, out pops a robin, a wren
perch on the end of my tongue
is a diving board

small bird bounces:

there are no stones
there is no rain
there are no names
only one woman.

"Some 7,000 people
living in Tochigi Prefecture sought compensation" —
only one name, only "one woman" —
" 'I don't know what to do,' one woman told local media"
"one woman had a surprise for the others"
"one woman was pinned against a wall"
"one woman in Kawasaki fled from Fukushima City"
"one woman was frantic that cesium was detected in her breast
        milk"
" 'My hair fell off,' one woman told me with tears"
"one woman stating, 'The government's decision-making process is
        wretched' "
"One woman's child became ill after the initial radiation"
"Not all of the families were able to come to Saitama together,
according to one woman from Iwaki"
"one woman (72) said, 'It's hard to lose our village' "
"one woman in her 30s, who evacuated to Nagano Prefecture"
"one woman demands that Shimizu live in an evacuation shelter"
" 'We want you to somehow get the nuclear plant under control,'
        one woman said"
"one woman said, 'I'm scared,' "
small bird bounces:

"I'm only left with worries about the future and health of my
       child," said Mako Tezuka, 45
"who would have thought the sun would come out?" said twig
       with Mako's name on it
and naming has a residue
as someone named after a Hardy heroine knows
as someone left out of the records shows

there are no stones
there is no rain
there are no names
only one woman

abandoned to the air
as a swimmer to the wave
these our names
back the way we came
through the forest
the road
the overground, street
the door
the fold
from sleep to wake
to the one name I have calling
the open water calling
the open throated thrush
and the robin and the wren
from the open skull pouring
and the stone and the rain

that never came, this and all
the alphabet guttered in the veins:
release.

VII

KING'S CROSS POND

'The installation aims to make us think about the relationship between nature and the urban environment – the permanence of buildings and the changing nature of undeveloped spaces.' – KING'S CROSS POND CLUB

drone lorry
drone camera
drone dog   tired air too early to

swim on the train
      on the tube
      on the platform blackberries / bougainvillea

swim in armpits
      in pheromones
      in bad suits / manners   folded sports news

getting to work
getting to WORK
by all means necessary – shove it blast it knock it shake it get it to
      WORK

                              I float. Small intimate pool of
strangers floating, chattering, buzzing. I float. Small intimate
likeminded lunatics. We float. Cold, cold in the bones of the morning

are stretching, are pulling out slouch, are cold in the morning of bones getting the body to WORK in the morning

is small. A kidney of water in the city, flat and still inside cement, DRY TARMAC, a lift going up, a train pulling across as I'm pulling across, a dragonfly, a buttercup still inside the building of a city

is finding its rhythm and feeling the body respond, become more of itself, because it is designed to move and is doing so. More and more it is its constituent parts – particular muscles, the pulse of the heart, the feet webbing, the eyes processing peeling the cells remembering storing and labelling this – plant; this – temperature; this – day, as a good one

rung out, slipped back, rejoin the upright. They are busy and loud and private. I am light and waterlilies. They stare. I am luminous. Goldfish. I flash and flare. And so they will have something to say when they get into work, "and there it was, this goldfish, walking down the street," flash flash a little live splash in the street in the fleet city drone.

Aegina

If at first light to swim until the sun
wrinkles gold and there to see a man
cradle a body in the sea
and try not to look too deeply
at the bunching of its limbs, the snap
they'd make if dropped, which hovers near
(a sonic vulture waiting) and the eyes
that disconnect with everything they meet
is to learn how to warm a body;
I would pick the whole Aegean Sea
up, lay it at your feet, let it wash through
the ward and swirl around your bed
until you thawed. The man passes. I stay.
It is a cold way to begin a day.

The Voice

Moon on sea, how you call to me, call to me.
Like vertigo I want to follow out
past the barriers of buoys; the fall
to me seems small compared with other doubts

as body falls back 45 degrees to float
upright towards a milky foam of sky.
I reach a quiet overlap of seas, few boats
pass here, too far to help if I should tire.

There I think I glimpse you, covered in fluid,
break out the stars in a bright astral birth,
showering confetti ever downward,
into dust all through the moving earth.

Is it land or sea beneath
my stretched body falling?
Is it your hand or water underneath
the moon calling.

Wallflowers

If water is baptism let it rain
rivers down your armies of taut veins
storming the heart. A battering of pear
scents air as I scull a memory where
you used to sell wallflowers — their yellows,
oranges, indecently gay, grown
through years of your worked dirt — I put the tired
ones in buckets to try to save them.
The day ducks high and low in a solemn
breaststroke, each lift a small christening.
You must feel my heart. It's vampiric
how I serve it up to you, each stroke
too quiet, can you hear me through water?
A girl, without a bucket to save you.

VIII

LLYN GWYNANT

All through the night I twitch my heart.
Swimming is a kind of hiccup
that jolts the body clean apart.
All through the night I twitch my heart;
tight contractions of sleep starts
break like waves pushing me up.
All through the night I twitch my heart.
Swimming is a kind of hiccup.

And though I wake from something deep,
the pull comes from the darkening lake.
It is not night, I did not sleep.
And though I wake from something deep,
it is not sleep my muscles heap
on bone but waves that gently break.
And though I wake from something deep,
the pull comes from the darkening lake.

Then always afterwards a calm
that flattens out the body's crease,
the water holds me in its palm
and always afterwards a calm,
a wash of mint and lemon balm
and wallflowers (once known as *heart's ease*);

then always afterwards a calm
that flattens out the body's crease.

IX

LLYN IDWAL

Soft pine breaks through the water where we pass.
The drop is gentle, yet the spine is tight:
a track of falling bone, of thickset night.
Thickets of sleep and rain in dreams fall fast
over the skeleton. Nothing dies here.
The light is endless; in strobes it passes
through the skin and lifts the pieces of
the body that can't lift themselves: the mind,
the memory and the rain that falls soundless
through our veins.

X

THE ENGLISH CHANNEL

For Edmund Hardy, Sam Solomon, Francesca Lisette, Jo Wilson, Florence Uniacke, Rosie Asquith, David Launchbury and an unnamed pelican.

'Titty, privately, was being a cormorant. This was not the sort of thing that she could very well talk of to John and Susan until she was sure that it was a success. So she said nothing about it. But she had seen that there were lots of minnows in the shallow water close to the shore. Perhaps there were bigger ones farther out, like the fish the cormorants had been catching yesterday. Titty had watched them carefully. The way they did it was to swim quietly and then suddenly to dive under water, humping their backs, keeping their wings close together, and going under head first.' — ARTHUR RANSOME, SWALLOWS AND AMAZONS

Directions for swim:
- **Convene on coast**
- **Receive a non-human identity (e.g. bird, fish, object)**
- **Enter sea under new identity**
- **Record memories of your non-human being**

(the records that follow are in the non-humans' own words)

Edmund, quietly, was being a cormorant.
It was risky. It was difficult. His arms were different. He turned his back. He flew crooked. He was becoming wrong. Limited pier.

Sam, quietly, was being at first a whale shark and then actually a horseshoe crab.
Tough! His circulatory system was suddenly something different. He didn't know what kind of blood he had now.

Fran, quietly, was being a fishing net.
Omnivorous, ghostly. The corners of her identity felt fragile, see-through, poked with light. She spread just sufficiently. There also came an urge to rescue, to catch, to grasp, to return. Ultimately, limpid.

Jo, quietly, was being a cormorant.
It was dangerous, an acute tumble, and he couldn't find his fish, he'd thought water was his element – flap – flap – shamed, crawled onto land – flap – croak – flap.

Florence, quietly, was being a plastic bottle cap.
She was abusive, whistling, deaf, vessel. She was cared but not cared for. She loathed her own resilience.

Rosie, quietly, was being a mackerel.
It was quite similar to her experience of being a human but with a much greater fear of losing her shoal and being eaten by a shark. She will be more thoughtful if she ever eats mackerel pâté.

David, quietly, was being a halibut.
Confusing. Powerless. Cold.

Someone, quietly, was being a pelican that wasn't happy, or a piece of litter.
They were unfussed but not willing/able to surrender completely.
They liked watching others be brave.

XI

PORTHMEOR

Record the sounds of species that human intervention has helped bring back from the brink of extinction. Play the recording into the sea.

Amur Tigers
Gray Whale
Southern White Rhinoceros
Black Rhinoceros
African Savannah Elephant
Mountain Gorilla
Saiga
Greater One-Horned Asian Rhinoceros
Golden Lion Tamarind
Takhi – Przewalski's Horse

The 5am worry of the shoulders makes
a w of the landscape waves
westerly break gaze already up
as surfers prowl with tigers in my palm wagtails
plunge into Atlantic's deep rhythms.
How can I soothe such harm
except with the sounds of other species
and the sleep that falls from us mingles
with the horse and the wrass and saiga
as the sea snail and mackerel pulse to gorilla
and the surfers meld bright bodies to the tide
as brine-bashed and salt-skinned I rise and I rise
and all of us glimpse a better way that we could be
living.

XII

THE DART

Anemone cloud over Dart,
tracking for a point of entry.
A walk is not a walk without a river.

Stepping stones, throughing roots,
yellow gorse flanks steepen to pink;
valley split open like a grapefruit.

Total immersion in hills: surround-sound air,
mist, buzzarding, moss, buttercupping, trees
brimming age into live memory banks.

Water drops off edge of stone to foam,
higher pools clear down to floor of purple campion, violet water —
                    boatmen skate —

the satisfaction of finding a spot deep enough to swim in needs its own
word,
signalling a joy at depth, like snorkelling without the snork; *kelling* —
eruption of eye over retina in slow pan of arrival, in spring kelling.
Entry is slip, unplanned into palette of oils,
limbs form brushstrokes, muddied in matter,

smell of earth and sadness at getting further from the river needs its

own word;
a de-connecting, de-spiriting, *de-kelling* –

but however quick the split between worlds opens up
however fast plates move beneath water breaks below planet
       heaves above
however soon the body is called back into building into posture
       into slump

there is a glimpse of an orange armband and an arm missing
from a waist that turned to see him watch as I pulled away
for the first time unaided into wildness,

unable to stand but able to swim (a river is not a river without him)

what the body buries the water returns, what the water buries the
       body burns
in slow sift of memory; keep kelling through the pages of the street,
       the lake, the body,

kelling in the middle of the room, the day, the core, keep kelling:
it is all yours, this open possibility.

Swimming is continuous, only the rivers are intermittent.

Printed in the USA
CPSIA information can be obtained
at www.ICGtesting.com
LVHW041132060224
771095LV00006B/256